Why Am I Here?

Dr. Theresa E. Scott

Cover Design: Donald Peart, Jr.
Contact Info: www.DonPeart.com

ISBN: 978-0615805009

Dedication

This book is dedicated to men and women everywhere who are or have been physically confined for a period of time. It is especially dedicated to the men at Eastern Correctional Institute, Westover, Maryland.

In addition, this book is dedicated to my husband, Chaplain Richard L. Scott, whom I've had the privilege of ministering with over an 18 year period to the men at Eastern Correctional Institute. His labor has not been in vain.

This book is also dedicated to *anyone* who has found themselves in an unlikely place in life where the last person you expect to encounter is God. May this book help you discover the mercy and grace extended to you by a loving God.

Acknowledgment

I want to thank my Lord for inspiring me for years to write this book to my brothers and sisters. This inspiration began over 30 years ago by writing letters to inmates and encouraging them in the faith. It is He Who has found me faithful to encourage those whom society has pushed aside. Their lives have impacted my life.

To my husband, Bishop Richard L. Scott, whose encouragement and inspiration constantly provoked me to good works. You have truly demonstrated the love of God to the unlovely. Over the years I have seen you pour your life out to these men as you have been steadfast in the work of the Lord.

To my church family at Grow In Grace Worship Center, Delmar, Maryland – you have always believed in me. Your faithfulness in prayer and intercession has far exceeded your petitions. It is because of that, this book has been manifested. To my daughter in the Lord, armor bearer, admin person, road warrior, Janae Fontaine – God truly sent you to me. There is no way I can do what I do without your invaluable expertise. You know how to make me look good!

Last, but *never* least, to my children – Jason and Amira. Thank you for sacrificing and sharing me with the Body of Christ. You are my legacy of godliness and righteousness in the earth.

Table of Contents

Foreword

Foreword by Chaplain J. L. Banks

A revelation springs out from these pages showing the futility of life in purposeless pursuits, as well as a uniqueness revealed to the distinctiveness of the individual. A simplistic yet profound case is made in this book for the reader to discover their purpose. Dr. Scott places a glowing light on why you are you, and the literal internment of life one will be destined to without discovering why they are here. To the person incarcerated inwardly or outwardly they should pause on every page and be enriched by the portrait drawn for them by God of their potential destiny.

Chaplain/Pastor J. L. Banks

Foreword by Dr Sandra Hayden

This book is a great read. A compass giving direction and guidance to its readers, helping them to find their purpose in life, and answering one of life's greatest questions. This book is a great resource for new believers and for anyone struggling with their identity. Thank you Dr. Theresa Scott.

Dr. Sandra Hayden
Dr. Sandra Hayden Ministries

Introduction

One Sunday I accompanied my husband to an evening service at the prison. He asked me to minister to the men since I hadn't been there in a while. I sought the Lord to give me a Word that would edify, comfort and exhort His people. I asked Him to allow all of us to have an encounter with Him.

As I stood before the men and looked at their faces, I saw men anointed and gifted by God. I saw men who wanted their lives turned around for the good. I saw men who never really wanted to end up in a place of physical confinement. The Holy Spirit spoke through me concerning God's original intent for their lives. I spoke of how God longed for them to find their purpose and destiny in Him. God's passion for them is to be a *new man.* These men have suffered misunderstandings and abuses of all types because they did not know their purpose. It's like looking for love in all the wrong places, while God has been there all along saying *'here I am.'*

I left the prison overloaded with compassion to help them see God in an unlikely place. Thus posing the question – **Why am I here?** God is not surprised at the paths we take in order to meet Him. He will take advantage of every event in our lives to reveal Himself to us. We are His people. He created us in His image and likeness. We belong to Him and He belongs to us. He wants to reveal Himself to us, but leaves us with the choice to accept Him.

It is God's desire that we choose Him because we want and need Him. God is so gracious to us. It is His goodness that leads us to repentance. (Romans 2:4) He loves and pursues us because that's what He wants to do. Nothing we do merits that. He has a way of loving the unlovely.

This book is intended to help you see that no matter where life leads you, God will always be there. Life has a way of putting you in some unlikely places. The majority of these places confine you. There is physical, mental and emotional confinement. You can be free outwardly, but confined inwardly. Your surroundings do not determine your confinement.

Christ came to set us free – spirit, soul and body. It is my prayer and desire that after reading this book you will be able to allow God's original intent to be manifested in your life. The past events in your life have taught you some valuable life lessons. Learn from those lessons and get on with your life no matter where you are. Break through your existing limitations by the power of the Holy Spirit. You may be confined, but the God in you is not. May you encounter Him right where you are. *"For whom the Son set free is free indeed."* (John 8:36)

Chapter One
Path of Life

Soul Searching

Why am I here? This question is asked in reference to where you presently find yourself in life. It leads you to seek an answer to your existence. It provokes dialogue with you – searching your soul and looking within.

Life has a way of putting you in places you never thought you would be. Even in your wildest imaginations, you never could have seen yourself in a place of utter confinement and restraints. Ending up in a place of confinement can prove to be a shock especially when you know you're too smart to end up like that. You've gotten away with a lot of things in the past. So you thought, until you got caught.

> *"Everyone must submit himself to the governing authorities, for there is no authority except that which God has established. The authorities that exist have been established by God. Consequently, he who rebels against the authority is rebelling against what God has instituted, and those who do so will bring judgment on themselves. For rulers hold no terror for those who do right, but for those who do wrong. Do you want to be free from fear of the one in authority? Then <u>do what is right</u> and he will commend you. For he is God's servant to do you good. But if you do wrong, be afraid, for he*

does not fear the sword for nothing. He is God's servant, an agent of wrath to bring punishment on the wrongdoer. Therefore, it is necessary to submit to the authorities, not only because of possible punishment but also because of conscience." (Romans 13:1-5, NIV)

Confinement and restraints are not solely limited to physical conditions. It also includes mental and emotional restraints as well. Have you ever felt like your mind is imprisoned? It's like a video being replayed in your head. It constantly replays past traumatic mental and emotional events. *Can somebody please push the stop button and eject this video??*

As you engage in searching your soul and looking within, you come to a point where you don't know who you are or where you're going. Life is bigger than you. It has gotten out of control. It's time to go to your Source – God.

"O Lord, you have searched me and you know me. You know when I sit and when I rise; you perceive my thoughts from afar. You discern my going out and my lying down; you are familiar with all my ways." (Psalm 139:1-3, NIV)

Life's Paths
Proverbs 14:12 (NIV) says *"there is a way that <u>seems right</u> to a man but in the end it leads to death."* It *seems right* to you. You rationalized in your mind that as long as it didn't

bother anybody, what was the harm? It's what you wanted to do – right? By looking back on your life, you realize you didn't always make the right choice. There were a lot of things you failed to take into consideration. You were driven by the moment, not by the consequences of the moment. It *seemed right* but ended up detrimental.

Sound Advice

Life is full of trials and errors. You try one way and it doesn't work. Try another way and it works. Others have experienced the same trials and made the same mistakes. You've heard their stories, observed their outcome, but believed it would never happen to you. Therefore, you ignored their advice because you just wanted to do your own thing.

Honestly, there are some paths in life we don't have to walk down. On these paths we run into counselors and advisors. They have vital intel on where we're going. They are like veteran scouts giving directions to avoid certain paths due to imminent danger. Do we take heed? We shouldn't have to question their advice. They know the terrain. Yet we go our own way and continue on to what *seems right* to us.

Chapter Two
Survival

Why am I here? causes you to reflect on how you survived the adversities of life. I'm fully persuaded we all came from dysfunctional families. Some had parents and some didn't. Parenting is on-the-job training. Your parents didn't take classes in parenting. It came by instinct. Some instincts were inadequate. Nevertheless, they did what they could to provide for you and in some cases made the best of a bad situation.

No one is actually prepared for *all* of life's challenges. Some had good parental upbringing with sound advice. Others received nothing. Think about how you were influenced by your own instincts to survive. On many occasions you were left on your own. Being left on your own opened the door to all types of influences and persuasions. Later you discovered life had a way of bringing out the best or worst in you. Then you really discovered your strengths and weaknesses. From this point on you sought ways to survive.

Survive means to live on – to remain alive or in existence. It also means to remain alive after the death of something or someone. It means to continue to exist. There are many levels of survival in order to exist. It's like the fight of your life without a trainer. You survived by whatever means necessary.

Think about your life. Think about what you lived through. You survived abandonment, ridicule and peer pressure. You also survived abuse, beatings, molestation and fear. The half of which most of us would have died in. Somehow you're still here! You still have some semblance of sanity, mental fortitude and physical stamina. You may not be 100%, but you're still here. You survived the worst of the worst.

Damaged Goods

Your life may not be looking too good right now, but it can be fixed. You may be damaged, but you're not destroyed. Damaged goods can be salvaged. All is not lost. You still have worth and value. You just need some repairs. That's why you're here in this place right now.

Your Manufacturer brought you here in order to give you a thorough inspection. Your life needed a diagnostic testing to see what parts are damaged and need to be replaced. Your life is salvageable. You still have some parts that are in good running order. Your heart (engine) is still running. Your body (frame) has some dents, but God can straighten them out and make you look good again.

8

Chapter Three
Actions Weighed

Why am I here? brings you to the issue of the choices you made and the consequences that followed it. This is when you realize what you and you alone did. No one put a gun to your head to make you do anything. You chose to do it of your own free will. Individuals like to blame others for their plight in life. The reality is that we all have a choice in the matter. The greater reality of the choice kicks in when the consequences of the choice comes to life. Choices always carry consequences.

Now if you were the victim of a circumstance, you had no choice in the matter. This is true to a certain extent. Victims do have a choice. The choice is how long will you remain a victim? How long will you continue to allow it to have power over you?

Choices

Webster's Dictionary defines *choice* as an act or power of choosing. It is a decision. *Choice* is an option, alternative, preference, selection, election. *Choice* suggests the opportunity or privilege of choosing freely. *Option* implies a power to choose that is specifically granted or guaranteed. *Alternative* implies a necessity to choose one and reject another or other possibilities. *Preference* suggests the guidance of choice by one's judgment or predilections.

Selection implies a wide range of choices. *Election* implies an end or purpose which requires exercise of judgment.

Choice suggests the opportunity or privilege of choosing freely. You are not coerced or influenced by anything or anyone. You choose what you want based on the opportunity being presented.

Option implies a power to choose that is specifically granted or guaranteed. Specific things are offered with specific guarantees. This is a power that has a right.

Alternative implies a necessity to choose one and reject another or other possibilities. You make a choice out of necessity – no options. Circumstances leave you with no options.

Preference suggests guidance of choice by one's judgment or predilections. This is a personal preference – you make the judgment call. Predilection is a strong liking deriving from one's temperament or experience. It's a personal like or dislike. This can be governed by your emotions.

Selection implies a wide range of choices. There are lots of things to choose from. This is a collection of choices. A range of choices can cause you to want everything!

Election implies an end or purpose which requires exercise of judgment. This choice is carefully selected. Many factors are included. It requires a lot of thought.

So you see choices come with consequences. It all boils down to thinking before acting. A thought can come to your mind in a flash. It's what you do with it that must be weighed.

Relationships

Relationships are a necessary part of life. We all have to interact with others – like it or not. Even so-called 'loners' have to interact. None of us had a choice in choosing the family we were born into. We didn't have a choice in who reared us. The choice had already been made.

As we grow we seek acceptance from others. Everyone seeks acceptance in one form or another. Social acceptance is normal. What makes it abnormal is the level of control and influence one is subjected to. Social acceptance should not require you to sell your soul in order to be accepted. Peer pressure can force you into something you don't want to do. Unfortunately people go to great lengths to please others at the risk of losing their identity and individuality.

Therefore, the choices made involved more than was realized. You are where you are right now based on the choices you made. Whether you were forced, coerced or influenced – you made the choice and the choice came with consequences.

Real Friends

Peer pressure and social acceptance leads us to consider friendships. What is a *friend*? The dictionary defines *friend* as one attached to another by affection or esteem. It is one that favors something.

Just because someone has similar likes and dislikes as you, does not mean they are your friend. Some are only acquaintances. They are in your life for a particular reason and season. People should qualify to be your friend. It's not that you are such a superior person. You need to value yourself. Take time with the people you encounter. A relationship should be developed over time. A trust should be earned. Their character should be proven to see who they really are. Think about who you have been connected to over the years. Did they prove to be friend or foe?

People say they got your back when they can't even be trusted with a secret. You find out who your friends really are when a crisis arises in your life. Life's crises have a way of revealing motives and commitments in relationships. Talk is cheap, but actions speak louder than words. We engraft people too quickly into our lives. We don't take time to allow a relationship to evolve into its real purpose. All relationships are not created equal! What a hard lesson to learn!!

Accountability

You understand now how choices carry consequences. Consequences take on accountability. Accountability is when you man-up or woman-up to what was done. This says *'I did it and I got to pay the price for what I did.'* When you get to this place, you see yourself for who you really are.

No one wants to admit that they are easily influenced. Reflect back on your life. You may have said you're your own person, but look how easy you were influenced. You chose to ignore all the warnings, stop signs and red flags. On the one hand, you felt the need to be governed by someone else's validation and opinion of you. You needed their acceptance. You soon discovered your own personal *neediness* from someone who was just as *needy* as you. They just happened to be one up on you. They figured out how to manipulate you to satisfy their own needs at your cost. On the other hand, you weren't influenced by anyone. You did your own thing to validate your own self. Either way, there has to be some accountability for your actions. You don't get to walk off into the sunset and leave your baggage for someone else to carry. Carry your own baggage!!

Chapter Four
Created By God

Why am I here? leads you to question the purpose of your existence. *Why was I created? What is God's intent for my life? Why is my life the way it is? Why do I have so many flaws and defects?*

It's amazing how we look to others to figure out who we are. We search for relationships, things and status to define our existence. Yet it never occurs to us to go to the One who created us. Why would you take a Volkswagen to a Ford dealership? You need the expertise and parts from a Volkswagen dealership. They know why and how that particular automobile is put together. Well, it's the same way with us. God created us. He's the only One who really knows why we were created. We go to friends, counselors, professionals, etc. to see what they say about us. We could save a lot of time and money by just going to God.

The Big Plan

God has big plans for your life. He created you with a purpose in mind. He knows exactly how your life is to be.

> *"I know what I'm doing. I have it all planned out –*
> *plans to take care of you, not abandon you, plans to give*
> *you the future you hope for. When you call on me, and*
> *when you come and pray to me, I'll listen. When you*

come looking for me, you'll find me. Yes, when you get serious about finding me and want it more than anything else. I'll make sure you won't be disappointed. God's Decree. I'll turn things around for you." (Jeremiah 29:11-14a, The Message)

In spite of your knowledge or lack thereof of God, He's the only One who can prosper you and give you hope and a future with no strings attached. He says *'come to the One who created you. I'll talk to you about what My purpose is for your life. Come to the Creator not the creature.'* God has your life mapped out. Don't exclude Him because of His ways – holy and righteous. He has the best life for you.

King David wondered about his life. He discovered something amazing about God.

Oh yes, you shaped me first inside, then out; you formed me in my mother's womb. I thank you, High God – you're breathtaking! Body and soul, I am marvelously made! I worship in adoration – what a creation! You know me inside and out, you know every bone in my body; you know exactly how I was made, bit by bit, how I was sculpted from nothing into something. Like an open book, you watched me grow from conception to birth; all the stages of my life were spread out before you. The days of my life all prepared before I'd even lived one day. Your thoughts – how rare, how beautiful! God, I'll never comprehend them! I couldn't even begin to count them – any more than I could count the sand of the sea." (Psalm 139:13-18, The Message)

Wow! This lets you know you are not a mistake in the earth. You were intricately created by God with a specific purpose in mind.

His Purpose

One of the greatest ambassadors and teachers in the Body of Christ is Dr. Myles Munroe (Bahamas Faith Ministries International, Nassau, Bahamas). In the early 1990's Dr. Munroe wrote books and did teachings on understanding your purpose and potential. He made a profound statement – *"where purpose is unknown, abuse is inevitable."* I will never forget it. It changed my life. When you don't know the purpose of a thing you will abuse it. You will use it for something it was never created for.

Take for example a baseball bat. The maker of the bat designed it to hit a baseball more accurately. He shaped the wood to be gripped properly by the batter in order to hit the baseball with great precision. The weight, length and circumference of the bat was taken into consideration. The bat is for the game of baseball – a sport. Its purpose is to be used by those who play the game of baseball – nothing else.

When the bat is used for purposes other than hitting a baseball, it has lost its purpose. The intended use is now being abused. Let's say someone other than a baseball player gets the bat. He looks at it for a purpose other than playing baseball. If the purpose of the bat is not clearly made known, that individual may see it as a weapon of destruction. Instead of using it for sport purposes, it's used to beat or destroy someone. The bat's purpose is to hit baseballs, not individuals. *Where purpose is unknown, abuse is inevitable.*

Original Intent

When you don't know the purpose of your life you will abuse it. God never created you to abuse yourself with drugs, alcohol, illicit or perverted sex, over-eating, under-eating, physical and mental negativity. When He created you He said it was *good.* (Genesis 1:31) You are fearfully and wonderfully made. (Psalm 139:14) God was very meticulous when He made you because you are one of a kind. You are unique. You have your own set of fingerprints that is not duplicated in another person. Even your personality is unique. There's nobody like you.

Your purpose is found in God. It has nothing to do with education, parents (known or unknown), job, profession, etc. It all has to do with God. He placed specific abilities in you. Take this opportunity now to go to Him to discuss your life.

God's original intent for mankind is found in Genesis – the book of beginnings. He said in Genesis 1:26 – *"Let us make man in our image, after our likeness: and let them have dominion over [earth]."* Then God said in verses 27-28 – *"So God created man in his own image, in the image of God created*

17

he him; male and female <u>created</u> he them." I don't see you being created in the image of your parents – only in the image of God. You may have your parents' tendencies (see Chapter 6), but you are not a reflection of them. You are a reflection of God.

In Genesis 1:26 you were *in* God because He spoke your existence *in* Himself. While *in* Him, He also *created* you (verse 27). Then God said in Genesis 2:7 – *"And the Lord <u>formed</u> man of the dust of the ground, and breathed into his nostrils the breath of life; and man became a living soul."* This is when He *formed* you in the natural (physical).

In the beginning God had a conversation about you being made like Him. Then He *created* you. *Create* means to make or to bring into existence. After He *created* you, He *formed* you. To *form* is to take on a recognizable shape. You started out *in* God. God brought you out of Himself! He then *formed* that image out of the ground. When He breathed life into what was *formed*, it came alive. He breathed Himself into what He *formed*. You are the offspring of that life.

He told man his purpose in Genesis 2:15 – *"And the Lord God took the man, and put him into the garden of Eden to dress it and to keep it."* Before man was formed in the ground, he already had purpose *in* him. Genesis 1:26 said he was to have dominion over the earth. God equipped him in Genesis 1:28 to be fruitful, multiply, replenish the earth, subdue it and have dominion.

God further defined man's purpose in Genesis 2:19-20 – *"And out of the ground the Lord God formed every beast of the field, and every fowl of the air; and brought them unto Adam to see what he would call them: and whatsoever Adam called every living creature, that was the name thereof. And Adam gave names to all...."* Look at how God made you!! You have untapped power and abilities *in* you and don't even realize it. The words you speak are powerful. That's why you have what you've been saying. You've been trying to dominate and subdue people when you should be dominating and subduing things. Things were never meant to dominate you.

This is God's original intent for mankind. The question is *what happened?* The answer is *sin.*

Analogy

Awhile back I ministered to a group of inmates at prison. I ministered to them about God wanting to make them into a *'new man.'* (Ephesians 2:15) The Lord had me to talk about their God given abilities. We used the life of a drug dealer as an example. The drug dealer has the ability to remember and know who sells drugs for him, how much the drugs are worth, and how much money is made in a specific amount of time. He keeps all these facts in his head – hardly nothing written on paper. He knows the quantity of drugs each person has been given to sell for him. He never loses track of who owes him money and how much they owe him. The drug dealer knows everybody by name. He has already calculated how much money he should have by the end of the day. Note: the majority of drug dealers never finished high school. Some never made it through middle school. Yet they have this mathematical ability to keep track of hundreds and thousands of dollars on a daily basis.

The drug dealer has his order of hierarchy and discipline to make the money. He has all of this business and corporate ability in him, but uses it in the wrong way. The drug dealer is blinded by fast money and lives for the moment. The addiction to the money causes him to use it wastefully – spending money on designer clothes, gold, silver, fancy cars, etc. There's nothing wrong with having those things, but first let's deal with the necessities of life.

The drug dealer never realizes that one day he may get caught and put in jail. At this point he doesn't even have enough sense to put some money away in case of an emergency. Out of all the money he has made, he doesn't even have money to make bail! He puts pressure on grandma, mom or some other family member to put their house up for collateral. They have to borrow money to make bail for him. But thousands of dollars have gone through his hands. Money wasted on designer clothes, only to end up in jail wearing a uniform labeled *DOC* (Department of Corrections). *Where purpose is unknown, abuse is inevitable.*

I told those men there are CEOs of corporations sitting in our midst – having their own companies and providing jobs for others. They have the ability to set up legal businesses without the fear of somebody putting a cap in them at any given moment.

Think about *you* right now. What's *in* you? God has placed Himself *in* you with abilities. There is a positive force *in* you that this world needs. There is some good in all of us. Tap into the good. Cultivate it. Bring it to the surface of your life. Understand it came from God. He put it *in* you to make a difference. It's never too late to use what God put *in* you.

Passion

God has placed in each of us a passionate desire to do a specific thing. Some discover it quicker than others. I'm not talking about a sensual or sexual passion. This passion is a strong enthusiasm or desire to help others. It's a drive to do good, make a positive difference. This passion goes beyond a talent. It's a gift. Let's say you have a gift to draw. That's wonderful. But can that gift be used to make a difference or help someone? Will your drawing have a positive or negative affect? You may be gifted to play an instrument – never had a formal music lesson. Playing the instrument is a natural for you. But can you play to soothe a soul, bring joy or teach others to play as well as you?

You will never be paid enough money to do what God has put in you. So stop looking in the direction of just making money. What you possess is priceless. It exceeds a monetary value. What you have is a gift. Freely you received, freely give.

Chapter Five
Spiritual Status

Why am I here? brings to light another question – *where do I go from here?* Then other questions arise – *why has my life been so hard, messed up and disappointing? Why, when I want to do right, I end up doing wrong? Why does it seem like bad things happen to me all the time?* We're going to take a side journey to clarify a few things.

Sin Issue

People don't like to talk about sin. When you talk about sin they equate it with judging. People get offended when you point out a *'wrong'* in their lives. They immediately go on the defense and say you're judging them. This is not judging. This is stating a fact concerning the spiritual state we were all born in. Let's define some words.

Iniquity – sin passed down from generation to generation

Trespasses – sins against others

Sin – missing the mark (according to the will of God)

The following scriptures describe our state of being before we were born. We had no choice in the matter. This sinful nature was handed down to all of us through the disobedience of Adam and Eve. Their disobedient act separated us from God. This was spiritual death. (Genesis 2:17)

> *"Therefore, as sin came into the world through one man, and death as the result of sin, so death spread to all men, [no one being able to stop it or to escape its power] because all men sinned."* (Romans 5:12, AMP)

> *"Behold, I was brought forth in [a state of] iniquity; my mother was sinful who conceived me [and I too am sinful].* (Psalm 51:5, AMP)

> *"And you [He made alive], by [your] trespasses and sins in which at one time you walked [habitually]. You were following the course and fashion of this world [were under the sway of the tendency of this present age], following the prince of the power of the air. [You were obedient to and under the control of] the [demon] spirit that still constantly works in the sons of disobedience [the careless, the rebellious, and the unbelieving, who go against the purposes of God]. Among these we as well as you once lived and conducted ourselves in the passions of our flesh [our behavior governed by our corrupt and sensual nature], obeying the impulses of the flesh and the thoughts of the mind [our cravings dictated by our senses and our dark imaginings]. We were then by nature children of [God's] wrath and heirs of [His] indignation, like the rest of mankind."* (Ephesians 2:1-3, AMP)

Sin separated us from God. No one was born saved.

The Struggle

Nobody has to point out whether you're living in sin or not. You know it. Everybody has a conscience. Within that conscience is the ability to distinguish right from wrong. We don't always do the good we want to do. There seems to be a struggle with good and bad. Let's see what the bible says about this struggle.

> *"For I do not understand my own actions [I am baffled, bewildered]. I do not practice or accomplish what I wish, but I do the very thing that I loathe [which my moral instinct condemns]. Now if I do [habitually] what is contrary to my desire, [that means that] I acknowledge and agree that the Law is good (morally excellent) and that I take sides with it. However, it is no longer I who do the deed, but the sin [principle] which is at home in me and has possession of me. For I know that nothing good dwells within me, that is, in my flesh. I can will what is right, but I cannot perform it. [I have the intention and urge to do what is right, but no power to carry it out.] For I fail to practice the good deeds I desire to do, but the evil deeds that I do not desire to do are what I am [ever] doing. Now if I do what I do not desire to do, it is no longer I doing it [it is not myself that acts], but the sin [principle] which dwells within me [fixed and operating in my soul]."* (Romans 7:15-20, AMP)

This is the struggle. You feel like you can't help yourself! You do good for a while, then BAM! – right back to the bad.

> *"So I find it to be a law (rule of action of my being) that when I want to do what is right and good, evil is ever present with me and I am subject to its insistent demands."* (Romans 7:21, AMP)

God understands all of this. That's why He sent His Son Jesus Christ to end the sin struggle. You are not stuck!

> *"O unhappy and pitiable and wretched man that I am! Who will release and deliver me from [the shackles of] this body of death? O thank God! [He will!] through Jesus Christ (the Anointed One) our Lord! So then indeed I, of myself with the mind and heart, serve the Law of God, but with the flesh the law of sin. Therefore, [there is] now no condemnation (no adjudging guilty of wrong) for those who are in Christ Jesus, who live [and] walk not after the dictates of the flesh, but after the dictates of the Spirit."* (Romans 7:24-25; 8:1, AMP)

I'm here to tell you that the struggle in this sinful state is over. It has been dealt with in the redemptive work of Jesus Christ. *There is no condemnation for those who are in Christ Jesus.* It's only over when you receive Christ into your life. There is hope!

Born Again

We had no choice in how we were born. *We do have a choice in how we will continue to live* once we have been informed and enlightened as to our present condition. Our nature is sinful until we take on a new nature which can only be done by being *'born again'* (second birth). We are all sinners, children of the devil until we become *born again* and receive Jesus Christ in our hearts. *"Marvel not [do not be surprised, astonished] at My telling you, you must all be born anew (again) (from above)."* (John 3:7, AMP) Your sinful nature can be changed. You're not stuck. You don't have to stay like you are. A change can take place. Aren't you sick and tired of being sick and tired? This drama in your life is old. Stop playing the scene. It's time for a new life!

Salvation

How many times were you told to get saved, give your life to Christ, call on Jesus, etc.? If you weren't asked these questions, you heard about it and probably didn't want anything to do with it. People told you to start going to church. You got locked up, scared, lonely and started going to church services or bible study. Or you visited a church feeling all broke up! You really needed help but didn't want anyone to say anything to you at that particular time. You weren't sure if you were ready for that *church* stuff. The majority of you know you would never be caught in a religious gathering because to you it implied weakness. Well, for whatever reason you refused, I hope this will help clear up some religious myths.

What's the purpose of salvation, being saved or born again? It has nothing to do with church. This is not a religious act. Going to church in and of itself can't save you. The purpose of salvation is to *change you*. This is what reconnects you to God (the Living God, Creator of the universe). This is how you enter into a relationship with God. I had to specify what God we're talking about because these days everybody calls on God. There are many gods in this world. I'm talking about the God who sent His only begotten Son, Jesus Christ, into the world to get mankind back to Him. (John 3:16) We can accept God, but some have a problem with Jesus Christ.

> *"For God sent not his Son into the world to condemn the world; but that the world though him might be saved."* (John 3:17)

> *"But what saith it? The word is nigh thee, even in thy mouth, and in thy heart: that is, the word of faith, which we preach; that if thou shalt confess with thy mouth the Lord Jesus, and shalt believe in thine heart that God hath raised him from the dead, thou shalt be saved. For with the heart man believeth unto righteousness; and with the mouth confession is made unto salvation. For the scripture saith, Whosoever believeth on him shall not be ashamed. For there is no difference between the Jew and the Greek: for the same Lord over all is rich unto all that call upon him. For*

whosoever shall call upon the name of the Lord shall be saved." (Romans 10:8-13)

"*Jesus said, 'You're absolutely right. Take it from me. Unless a person is born from above, it's not possible to see what I'm pointing to – to God's kingdom.' 'How can anyone,' said Nicodemus, 'be born who has already been born and grown up? You can't re-enter your mother's womb and be born again. What are you saying with this 'born-from-above' talk?' Jesus said, 'You're not listening. Let me say it again. Unless a person submits to this original creation – the 'wind hovering over the water' creation, the invisible moving the visible, a baptism into a new life – it's not possible to enter God's kingdom. When you look at a baby, it's just that: a body you can look at and touch. But the person who takes shape within is formed by something you can't see and touch – the Spirit – and becomes a living spirit. So don't be so surprised when I tell you that you have to be 'born from above' – out of this world, so to speak. You know well enough how the wind blows this way and that. You hear it rustling through the trees, but you have no idea where it comes from or where it's headed next. That's the way it is with everyone 'born from above' by the wind of God, the Spirit of God.'*" (John 3:3-8, The Message)

Born again means you take on a new nature. Your old sinful nature dies. You now take on the nature and characteristics of God. You are no longer a child of the devil. Your spirit has now become born of God. This puts you back in right standing with Him. You reconnect with Him. No more separation due to sin.

Holy Spirit

Being born again is the first step. It gets you into the kingdom of God. But you need more. You need *power* to stay saved. Jesus' disciples knew about Him. They accepted Him into their lives. They saw His miracles and listened to His teachings. They were acquainted with Him. (Initially that's how we are in our acceptance of Him.) But something was missing. They needed *power*.

> *"But ye shall receive power, after that the Holy Ghost is come upon you: and ye shall be witnesses unto me both in Jerusalem, and in all Judea, and in Samaria, and unto the uttermost parts of the earth."* (Acts 1:8)

This *power* was sent to the disciples on the day of Pentecost according to Acts 2:1-4. Now when they spoke about Christ it was different. Their witness and testimony had *power*. It was more effective. It carried more weight. So it is with you. You need the *power* of the Holy Spirit to do likewise in your life.

The Holy Spirit is also the Spirit of Truth. His other purpose is to *conform* you into the image of Christ, but you must cooperate and let Him do His job. *"For those God*

29

foreknew he also predestined to be conformed to the likeness of his Son, that he might be the firstborn of many brothers." (Romans 8:29, NIV) Allow the Holy Spirit to *conform* you to the likeness of Jesus Christ. He is the Spirit of Truth. He comes to give you the truth of God's Word. He brings revelation and enlightenment. (Ephesians 1:17-18)

Renewal of the Mind

Let us go on in Christ. Now that your spirit has changed and is of God, your mind and body still have sin tendencies. In your spirit you are connected to God, but not your mind and body. Your mind has to be renewed – changed – according to the Word of God. This is where people get stuck and confused. People are told when they give their life to Christ everything will be fine. Christ will turn your life around and all will be well. They make it sound like something magical takes place with no effort from the individual. It's implied that Jesus is going to do everything for you. Yes, you have a new spirit made in the likeness of God. This gets you back to your original place in God. BUT your mind has to be renewed. *This is your responsibility, not God's!*

"Therefore if any man be in Christ, he is a new creature: old things are passed away; behold, all things are become new." (2 Corinthians 5:17) The scripture says *"all things are become new." Become* is a process. The process now involves thinking different according to the Word of God. Old mental and physical habits must be changed and broken by the

power of God's Word. Your mind must be changed in light of God's Word.

> "Do not be conformed to this world (this age), [fashioned after and adapted to its external, superficial customs], but be transformed (changed) by the [entire] renewal of your mind [by its new ideals and its new attitude], so that you may prove [for yourselves] what is the good and acceptable and perfect will of God, even the thing which is good and acceptable and perfect [in His sight for you]." (Romans 12:2, AMP)

Word of God

You will never successfully get rid of old habits and thoughts until you *replace* them with new ones which is by the Word of God. This means you are going to have to study God's Word and *do* what it says. Feed your mind the Word of God. You experience the new by experiencing the Word.

The Bible is not just a religious book, it is your life. Feed your mind with the Word like you feed your body food. The battle is in the mind. The devil fights your belief system. He challenges and twists what God says to you. You fight him with the Word, not your feelings or fists. Your battle is spiritual.

You are more than a conqueror by the sake of the Word. God's Word is spiritual. You are spiritually victorious because of what the Word says. But you must believe and practice what you read and study. The mind and body must be disciplined according to the Word of God. Old habits have to be broken and replaced. If you continue to do the same things, you will always have the same results. God's ways in your life guarantee changes for a better life.

Chapter Six
Discovering God In A Strange Place

Why am I here? Well, it took five chapters to understand the purpose for this question. We discussed soul searching, pondered on the paths of life, reflected on the choices made, understood surviving just to live. You read about God's original intent for you. You have been enlightened on your original sinful state, shown how to come out of it by being born again. You have had the purpose of the Holy Spirit explained to you and understood the importance of renewing your mind.

God created you for a specific purpose. He has a grand and wonderful plan for your life. You are not a mistake in the earth. He created you with purpose and value. No matter what you've done in life (good or bad) God's plan for you is still in effect. His hand of righteousness is on you. (Psalm 139:5) Nothing will change His mind about His will for your life. He knows the way you should go. (Job 23:10)

The place where you discover Him may be strange, but He's not. It's not the place of your discovery, it's Who you discover. God is committed to you. You are His child and He is your Father. He is a loving Father. He will not force His will on you. He wants you to accept and serve Him willingly. When you discover the Father, you discover His Son Jesus Christ.

Your heavenly Father is committed to an eternal relationship with you. He sent His Son to bring you to Him. I'm not appealing to you to *try* Jesus. That would imply an on and off relationship based on likes and dislikes. My appeal to you is to allow the One who created you to work out His plan in you. That can only happen when you unreservedly give Him your life. If you have given Him your life in the past and strayed away or willfully walked away, He's waiting for your return.

There is a program on T.V. called the Discovery Channel. On that program credible facts are given on a range of topics. You receive visual insight and understanding. The program holds your interest because of the information given. You become knowledgeable about something you didn't know before. There's something about information and knowledge that empowers you. It gives you confidence.

Discovering God is similar. You won't find Him on the Discovery Channel, but the Holy Spirit will draw you to Him. He will reveal the Father and the Son to you. The Spirit of Truth will dispel all lies and myths you had about God. He will introduce you to the Son Jesus Christ. Jesus Christ will point you to the Father (Creator). What a wonderful discovery!!

Why am I here?
❖ To come grips with me and my life
❖ Accept accountability for my actions

- ❖ To get a reality check on who are my real friends
- ❖ Realize I need help from someone greater than me – I need help from God
- ❖ To receive Christ in my life and connect with my Creator
- ❖ To be willing to live my life the way God intended it to be
- ❖ To get to know God for who He is and not just for what He can do for me
- ❖ To know I have another chance to do good and make my life count

"Are you tired? Worn out? Burned out on religion? Come to me. Get away with me and you'll recover your life. I'll show you how to take a real rest. Walk with me and work with me – watch how I do it. Learn the unforced rhythms of grace. I won't lay anything heavy or ill-fitting on you. Keep company with me and you'll learn to live freely and lightly." (Matthew 11:28-30, The Message)

Prayer

Father I come to You – my Creator. I come by Your great mercies. I confess to You that I have transgressed against people. I have disobeyed You and the laws of the land. I willingly did these things knowing it was wrong. I realize I cannot hide anything from You because You know all things. I come clean with You out of the sincerity of my heart. I ask You to forgive me for living a life contrary to Your will and Your way. I realize I was born in sin and shaped in iniquity. I believe Jesus died and rose again and is now seated at the right hand of the Father. I ask that the blood of Jesus Christ cleanse me from all unrighteousness. Wash me and make me whole.

I give You my life. Cause me to be born again. I want the nature of my heavenly Father. I renounce the hidden things of darkness in me. I want to be born again. I ask Jesus to come into my heart and live in me. Translate me now out of darkness and bring me into the marvelous light of Jesus Christ.

Now that I'm born again, I need the help of the Holy Spirit to conform me into the image of Christ Jesus. Fill me with the Holy Spirit. I yield to you. Holy Spirit take control of me now. Father, draw me into Your Word. May the Spirit of wisdom and revelation in the knowledge of You be released in me so I can know you better. Order my steps in your Word so that iniquity will not have dominion over me. Teach me how to renew my mind according to Your Word. Help me to be a doer and not just a hearer of the Word.

Thank You Father for saving me! Thank you for filling me with the Holy Spirit. I make a decision to discipline myself to study and do your Word daily. This is vital to my continued deliverance and growth in You. In Jesus' name, Amen!

<u>Prayer Scripture References</u>:
Romans 10:9-13
Psalm 119:133
Colossians 1:13-14
John 14:16-17, 26
1 John 1:9
Psalm 51:5
John 3:3
Ephesians 5:18
Ephesians 1:17
Hebrews 9:22
1 Peter 1:18-19
Romans 12:2
James 1:22-25
Psalm 139:1-16
2 Corinthians 4:2
2 Timothy 2:15

References

Webster's Seventh New Collegiate Dictionary, based on Webster's Third New International Dictionary, Copyright © 1979 by G. & C. Merriam Company, Publishers, Springfield, Massachusetts, U.S.A.

About the Author

Dr. Theresa E. Scott is a prophetess and teacher to the Body of Christ. She has been saved 35 years. She ministers with her husband (Bishop Richard L. Scott) at Grow In Grace Worship Center, Delmar, MD (www.gigwc.com).

Dr. Scott received her Doctor of Divinity degree from Spirit of Truth Institute, Richmond, VA, Master of Christian Education and Bachelor of Biblical Studies degrees from H.E. Wood Bible Institute & Theological Seminary, Alexandria, VA.

The Holy Spirit teaches through her with clarity and practical revelation of God's Word. She is anointed in intercession and spiritual warfare. God has favored her in ministering in workshops, conferences and revivals. She always comes with a *"Word for the house."*

Dr. Scott's ministry is world-wide, carrying her to South Africa and mission trips to Nairobi, Kenya. She ministers in open air crusades and conferences with signs and wonders following. *"I keep asking that the God of our Lord Jesus Christ, the glorious Father, may give you the Spirit of wisdom and revelation, so that you may know him better."* (Eph. 1:17, NIV)

She has an anointed women's ministry which exhorts, edifies and encourages women – setting them free to live a genuine balanced life in Christ. She has a passion for women to accept themselves and walk in the power of their individuality.

Dr. Scott is the Founder and President of Humble Time International Women's School of Ministry, Inc., Salisbury, MD (www.humbletime.org). This school is established to raise the standard of kingdom principles in the lives of women in all areas of ministry. The curriculum consists of empowerment and strong character building classes. She is featured daily on a local radio broadcast sponsored by Humble Time – *Perfecting Moment* – empowering God's kingdom one minute at a time.

Dr. Scott is the President of Time Wize Consulting, Inc., Salisbury, MD (www.timewizeconsulting.com). This business meets the needs of individuals and businesses to better manage their time. This is done through workshops and motivational speaking. *"There is a time and a season for every activity under the sun."* (Eccles. 3:1)

Contact Information:

Dr. Theresa E. Scott
P. O. Box 2083
Salisbury, MD 21802
Email: prphttee@comcast.net * humbletime@comcast.net